It's me... a Lion

Om KIDZ
An imprint of Om Books International

First Published in 2019 by

Om Kidz | Om Books International

Corporate & Editorial Office
A-12, Sector 64, Noida 201 301
Uttar Pradesh, India
Phone: +91 120 477 4100
Email: editorial@ombooks.com
Website: www.ombooksinternational.com

Sales Office
107, Ansari Road, Darya Ganj
New Delhi 110 002, India
Phone: +91 11 4000 9000
Email: sales@ombooks.com
Website: www.ombooks.com

ISBN: 978-93-86410-42-9

Printed in India

10 9 8 7 6 5 4 3 2 1

Contents

Who are you? 04
Where do you live? 05
What are your babies called? 06
When do cubs start hunting? 07
What do you like to eat? 08
Is it true that only lionesses hunt? 09
How do you carry out a hunt? 10
How big are you? 11
What colour is your fur? 12
What is your lifespan? 13
Why do you roar? 14
How do you communicate? 15
Who all are there in your family? 16
How fast can you run? 18
Do male cubs leave their pride? 19
Who are Mountain lions? 20
Where are Mountain lions found? 21
Activity time 22-24

WHO ARE YOU?

We are powerful and agile creatures. We belong to the cat family, Felidae. We have a big head, a strong body and short legs. We are most active during the night.

Scientific Name

Panthera leo

WHERE DO YOU LIVE?

We are found across Asia, Africa and Europe. We can adapt to various kinds of environments including the savannas, grasslands and dense scrubs.

Lions Live in Prides

We live in a group known as a 'pride'. The members of the pride mostly spend their day roaming around in several scattered groups, which may come together to hunt or eat. A pride comprises of many generations of lionesses, their cubs and not more than two lions. A group may have as few as 4 or as many as 37 members.

WHAT ARE YOUR BABIES CALLED?

Our babies are called cubs. When the cubs are born, they are blind and have a thick coat with dark spots. These spots disappear as the cubs grow older. They start following their mothers when they are about three months old.

WHEN DO CUBS START HUNTING?

Our cubs start hunting by the time they are 11 months old but they cannot survive on their own until they are two years of age.

Litter Size

The litter size can vary between one to six cubs.

WHAT DO YOU LIKE TO EAT?

We are carnivores and we prey on a large variety of animals, ranging from rodents and baboons to water buffaloes and hippopotamuses. However, we mostly hunt medium- and large-sized animals including deer, zebras, antelopes and wildebeests.

IS IT TRUE THAT ONLY LIONESSES HUNT?

No. Even though lionesses are known to do most of the hunting, the lions take their share from the kill. Lions are also skilled hunters and in some areas they hunt for themselves regularly. The nomadic males always hunt for their own food.

Territorial Defence

Lions defend the territories of their pride while lionesses hunt.

A new word to learn

Nomad - one who moves from place to place

HOW DO YOU CARRY OUT A HUNT?

We hide behind bushes and stalk our prey, and then leap forward and pounce on it. The entire group joins in to feast on the prey.

An adult lion can consume over 34 kg of meat in a single meal and then rest for a whole week before hunting again.

Lazing Around

We spend our day resting or roaming around the forest. We spend only 2 to 3 hours hunting and then rest for about 20 hours a day.

HOW BIG ARE YOU?

A fully grown lion is around 1.8 to 2.1 m long and has a 1 m long tail. Lions are about 1.2 m in height and weigh almost 170 to 230 kg. A lioness usually has a body length of around 1.5 m and a height of 0.9 to 1.1 metres. Lionesses weigh about 120 to 180 kg.

WHAT COLOUR IS YOUR FUR?

We have a tuft on our tail tip which is usually darker than the rest of our coat.

Our fur varies from buff yellow to orangish-brown, or from silvery gray to dark brown.

Our mane and fringe are very dark and they make us appear extremely majestic.

WHAT IS YOUR LIFESPAN?

We rarely survive for more than 8 to 10 years, when in the wild. This is mainly because we are hunted by humans or attacked by other lions. However, in captivity, we can live up to 25 years.

Endangered Species!

Due to hunting and loss of habitat because of human activities, lions are now an **endangered** species.

A new word to learn

Endangered - at the risk of extinction

WHY DO YOU ROAR?

We mark our territories by roaring and scent marking. Our roars can be heard in the evening before our night-time hunting. We also roar when we wake up at dawn.

Loudest of All

A lion's roar is the loudest of any big cat species and can be heard from almost five miles away.

HOW DO YOU COMMUNICATE?

We communicate through a range of behaviours. We show our affection by rubbing heads, nuzzling and licking each other. We make various sounds such as snarls, hisses and purrs.

Night Vision

We have excellent night vision because we are six times more sensitive to light than human beings. This helps us to hunt at night.

WHO ALL ARE THERE IN YOUR FAMILY?

Hello, I am a lynx. I am known for my tufted ears, which give me a unique appearance.

Hi, I am a serval. I am known for my speed.

Hi, I am a tiger. I am the largest member of the cat family.

Hi, I am a jaguar. I am mostly found in swamps and wooded regions.

Hello, I am a leopard and I am an agile climber.

Hi, I am a snow leopard. I am native to the rugged and snowy mountains of Central Asia.

Hi, I am a domestic cat and I am the smallest member of the cat family.

HOW FAST CAN YOU RUN?

We can run at a speed of 50 miles per hour and we can leap as far as 11 metres.

National Symbol

Lions are known to signify pride, strength and courage. Hence several countries across the world consider the lion as their national symbol.

Ashoka Stambh
National Symbol
India

Coat of Arms
National Symbol
Netherlands

The Lion Head
National Symbol
Singapore

DO MALE CUBS LEAVE THEIR PRIDE?

Yes. Once male cubs attain full growth, they are forced to move out of their pride. Then they either join other prides or wander alone as nomads.

The Lonely Nomad

It has been observed that many adult lions remain nomads for life.

WHO ARE MOUNTAIN LIONS?

The Mountain lion, also known as the puma or panther, is a member of the cat family. Mountain lions are big cats who are brownish in colour.

Nocturnal Creatures

Pumas are **nocturnal** creatures but also are active at dusk and dawn.

A new word to learn

Nocturnal - active at night

WHERE ARE MOUNTAIN LIONS FOUND?

Elusive Beings

Pumas are very **elusive** beings and prefer avoiding people. This is why they avoid agricultural areas, flatlands, and other similar habitats.

We are found in diverse habitats such as forests, desert scrub, chaparrals and swamps.

A new word to learn

Elusive - difficult to find

Activity Time

3D Paper Lion

Things You'll Need

- Thick yellow and orange craft paper
- Scissors
- Glue stick
- Black marker
- Pencil

Cut the yellow paper in half and then fold it into half. Cut out a U-shape.

01

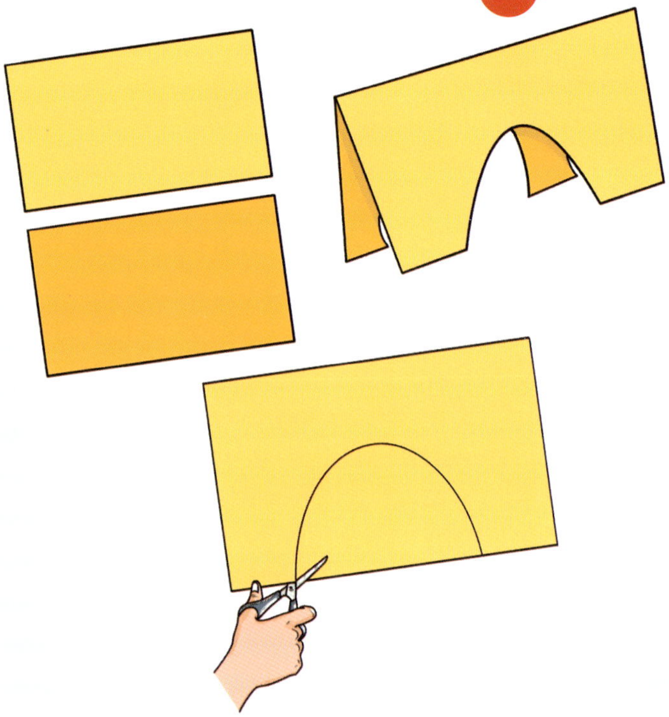

02

Mark 1/2 and 1/4 segments on the side of the head and tail of the paper. Cut off 3/4 length for the head.

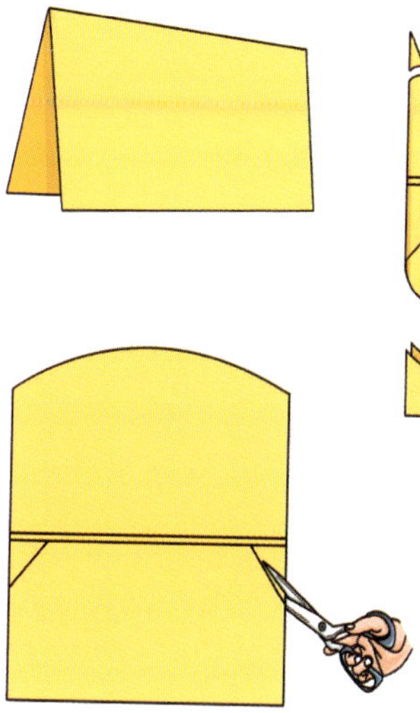

03

Fold the paper kept aside for the head of the lion, into half. Next, cut out slits for ears. Fold the head and trim the ears and chin to get a round edge.

04

Cut out 11 little triangles using orange paper. Glue the triangles around the face. Cut out the nose and eyes of the lion. Draw the eyeballs using a black marker.

05

Glue the eyes and nose to the face. Cut out a tail for the lion, using yellow paper. Cut out a tail-end with orange paper and glue it to the tail. Attach the tail and head to the body of the lion.
Your 3D Lion is ready.

The lion is hungry.
Help it reach the meatloaf!